Omar & Hana

Ramadan Activity Book

This Activity Book Belongs to _____

T0020400

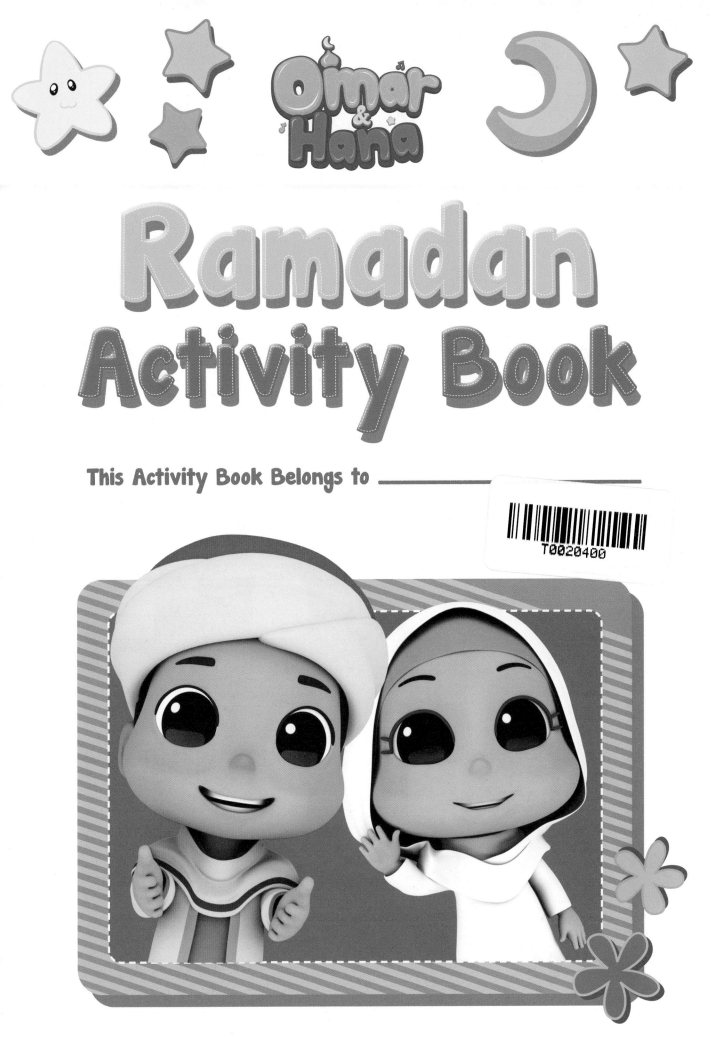

astro — DIGITAL DURIAN

THE RAMADAN MOON

Yay! The Ramadan Moon is here! A new moon marks the beginning of a new month. The new moon is usually very hard to see with the naked eye.

Can you help Omar and Hana find the Ramadan moon?

Tick one picture that shows the new moon.

Did you know?

Did you know that the months in the Islamic calendar follow the movement of the moon not the sun?

THE NEW MOON DUA!

Alhamdulilah! The new moon has been sighted. We bid farewell to Shaban and welcome the Holy month of Ramadan.

Let's learn the dua we pray on sighting the new moon. Pray and memorise the dua below with an adult until you know it without looking in the book.

اللَّهُمَّ أَهِلِهِ عَلَيْنَا بِالْأَمْنِ وَالْإِيمَانِ، وَالسَّلَامَةَ وَالْإِسْلَامَ، وَالتَّوْفِيقَ لِمَ تُحِبُّ رَبَّنَا وَتَرْضَى رَبَّنَا وَرَبُّكَ الله.

Allahumma Ahhilhu 'Alayna bi'l-Amni wa'l-Imani wa'l-salamati wa'-Islami wa'l-Tawfiqa Lima tuhibbu Rabbana wa-Tarda, Rabbuna wa-Rabbuka Allahu.

O Allah, let the crescent moon appear over us with security and Iman; with peace and Islam; and with ability for us to practice such actions which You love. (O Moon) My creator and your Creator is Allah.

Did you know?

Around the world, Ramadan starts on different days as the new moon is seen on different days in different countries.

IT'S TIME TO DECORATE!

It's time to celebrate the holiest month of our calendar!

Decorate your very own special Ramadan banner and balloons! Maybe you can write "Ramadan Mubarak" in the bunting? What else will you add?

Remember to make it colourful by using stickers and colouring pencils!

5

TIME FOR SUHOOR!

It is time for Suhoor!
Hana needs help choosing what she will eat before she begins her fast.
What should she eat?

Draw and colour what you think Hana should eat for suhoor. Remember she needs lots of healthy food to stay full and energised throughout the day!

Stuck?
Have a look at these images to help you!

Helpful Hadith!

The Prophet Muhammad (SAW) said:
"The best Suhoor for the believer is dates."

(Abu Dawood 2345)

SUHOOR SPELLING!

Suhoor is the meal we eat before we begin our fast. We must eat this before the sun rises.

Fill in the missing letters to spell the words below. Use the description to help you guess what they are.

W _ T _ R
You must drink lots of this before your fast to keep you hydrated.

W _ D _
So we are clean for Salah.

D _ A
We pray one before we begin our suhoor meal.

B _ N _ N _
A yummy fruit that gives us lots of energy. Also monkeys love to eat them!

Helpful Hadith!
The Prophet Muhammad (SAW) said: "Eat Suhoor, for in Suhoor there is blessing."
(Bukhari 1923 & Muslim 1095)

F _ J _
The first salah of the day which is prayed just before the sun rises.

WUDU WASH

Help Omar make wudu before Salah.

Number each part of the body in the correct order for wudu.
Ask a grown up to help you if you are stuck!

Helpful Hadith!

Did you know the Prophet (SAW) said "Wudu helps wash away sins." (Sahih Muslim 0475)

THE MASJID MAZE!

Help Omar get to the mosque in time for Fajr through the maze. Which way is correct?

START →

FINISH

Did you know?
It is Sunnah to walk a different way home after each Salah.

IT'S TIME FOR SALAH!

Can you help Omar and Hana with Salah times?
Using the timetable below, draw the hands on the
clock faces for each Salah.

Salah	Time
Fajr	6:15 am
Zuhr	1:30 pm
Asr	6:30 pm
Maghrib	7:45 pm
Isha	9:30 pm

Fajr

Zuhr

Asr

Maghrib

Isha

Did you know?
Salah around the world is at different times. Why do you think this is?

QIBLA CHRONICLES

Muslims pray Salah facing the Kaaba, which is in Makkah. This is our Qiblah.

Can you help Omar and Hana find the Kaaba?
Draw a line from Omar and Hana's house in Malaysia,
to Makkah, where the Kaaba is in Saudi Arabia.

Did you know?
The first Qiblah was towards Masjid Al Aqsa?
It was also the first Masjid that Salah was ever
performed in by the Prophet Muhammad (SAW).

THE BEAUTY OF SALAH

Match the questions on the left to the answers on the right.

WHO?

Salah means 'to pray' in Arabic. It is a special prayer where Muslims pray and do different actions.

WHAT?

Salah was given as a gift to the Prophet Muhammad (SAW) and his ummah (which is us!) by Allah.

WHERE?

Salah is prayed five times a day but there are some other special Salahs too, such as Tarawih, which is prayed every night in Ramadan.

WHY?

Salah can be prayed anywhere! As long as the area is clean and facing the Qiblah. Most Muslims pray at the Mosque or at home.

WHEN?

Salah is important because it lets us speak to Allah. It is also the second pillar of Islam.

Did you know?

"The key to Paradise is prayer, and the key to prayer is ablution."

(Sunan al-Tirmidhi 4)

14

FOCUSING WHILST FASTING

Tick the thoughts and actions Omar & Hana should try to focus on during their fast. Fasting during Ramadan is compulsory for those who can.

Did you know?

Did you know it is good practice to read one full Quran during the month of Ramadan.

A HELPFUL HAND

Did you know that helping people is a Sunnah? What six things can Omar & Hana do at home to help their parents? Have a grown-up help you if you get stuck.

1. Clean the _____

2. Wash the _____

3. Tidy the _____

4. Throw away the _____

5. Help mum with _____

6. Help dad with _____

Helpful Hadith!

"The best of people are those that bring the most benefit to the rest of mankind."

(Al-Mu'jam al-Awsa, 6/139)

RAMADAN WORD SEARCH

Help Omar & Hana find words relating to Ramadan.
Look, they have already found one for you!

S	U	H	O	O	R	O	M	Z	F
I	O	R	S	E	A	G	A	X	X
F	F	A	F	T	M	N	S	R	N
I	W	T	V	T	A	O	J	Q	X
M	Q	R	A	R	K	C	I	C	B
B	F	I	U	R	L	P	D	K	D
K	T	Q	H	A	N	N	U	S	T
K	A	I	K	Q	G	M	V	X	N
Q	F	M	X	O	B	J	F	E	V
G	M	E	L	B	B	Y	G	Y	B

QURAN
SUHOOR
IFTAR
MASJID
SAWM
SUNNAH

Did you know?
All these words are
very important for
Ramadan. Do you know
what they mean?

17

DOT TO DOT!

Join the dots in order to reveal a
super special place.
Have you been to one of these?

Did you know?

There are different reasons
we visit the Masjid. Why did
you attend the Masjid?

DAILY DUAS

Did you know most actions need a dua?
Match the dua with the correct action
below by drawing a line.

1   بِسْمِ اللّٰهِ وَعَلَى بَرَكَةِ اللّٰهِ

2   أَعُوذُ بِاللهِ مِنَ الْخُبْثِ وَالْخَبَائِثِ

3   اللَّهُمَّ بِاسْمِكَ أَمُوتُ وَأَحْيَا

4   سُبْحَانَ الَّذِي سَخَّرَ لَنَا هَذَا وَمَا كُنَّا لَهُ مُقْرِنِينَ وَإِنَّا إِلَى رَبِّنَا لَمُنْقَلِبُونَ

Did you know?
Duas are important as they remind us of Allah and his Mercy throughout the day.

IFTAR PLATTER

Omar & Hana have helped their mum create yummy food for iftar today!
Spot 5 differences between the two platters.

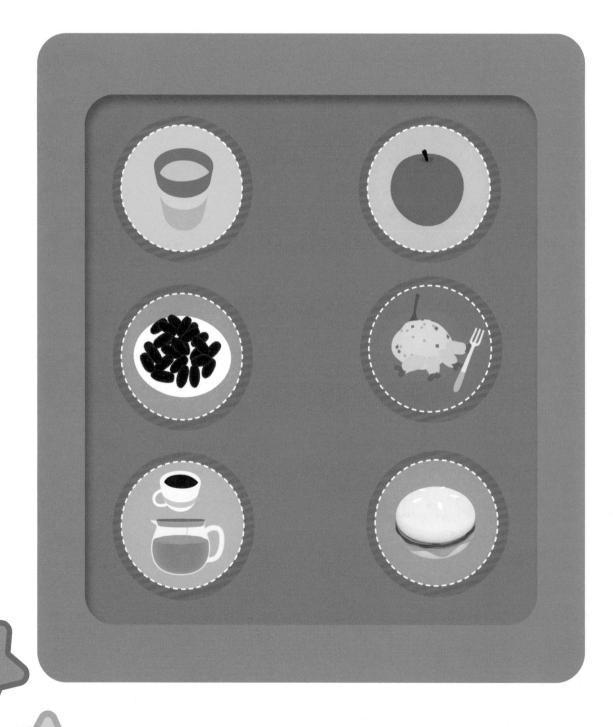

Did you know?
The dua for opening fast is different to the dua before eating?

IT'S NEARLY TIME FOR IFTAR!

Did you know that the time before Iftar is very special? Allah loves to listen and accept the wishes of those who make Dua during this time.

What things have you wished for before you break your fast? Draw or write it in the speech bubbles below.

Helpful Hadith!

The Prophet Muhammad (SAW) said "The breath of someone fasting is more sweeter than musk (one of the sweet smells of Jannah)" (Sahih al-Bukhari 5927)

WHAT DID YOU EAT FOR IFTAR?

Draw in the plate below what you ate for iftar today. Add some colour to it too!

Did you know?
It's Sunnah to share your food. Who did you share with today?

DAILY REFLECTION

What good deeds did you do today?

In the box below write or draw three good deeds you completed today.

1. _____

2. _____

3. _____

Did you know?
By helping others, you will receive lots of rewards from Allah!

TO FAST OR NOT TO FAST?

Some people do not have to fast. If you are sick, old, or a small child "like Hana!" you do not have to fast. Also if you are a traveller you do not have to fast too.

Draw a circle around the people who do not have to fast. Hint! There are four answers you need to find!

Helpful Hadith!

The Prophet Muhammad (SAW) said: "Allah is kind and he loves kindness in all matters."
(Sahih Bukhari 6528)

DESIGN A SALAH MAT

Can you help Omar & Hana design a colourful Salah Mat? Design and colour the Salah Mat below. Are you stuck? Ask an adult to show you Salah Mat's you have at home for some inspiration, or have a search on the internet!

DAILY DUAS

Hana loves to make dua! A dua is a wish you make to Allah that you really want to come true.
You can make dua for others too like your family, friends and the whole Ummah!

Write or draw what you wish for in the boxes below.

Family

I make dua that...

_____

_____

_____

Friends

I make dua that...

_____

_____

_____

Did you know?

One of Allah's names is "As-Samee", which means he hears everything, no matter how quietly you say it! This means Allah listens to **ALL** our duas!

The Ummah

I make dua that...

_____

_____

_____

_____

RAMADAN RIDDLES

Help Omar & Hana solve the riddles below.

Read the information and write what you think is being described.

1 The prophet Muhammad (SAW), used to eat me first when breaking his fast. What am I?

2 I am the most important month in the Islamic calendar. The Quran was revealed during this month too. What am I?

3 I am celebrated by Muslims all over the world at the end of this month once we see the new moon. What am I?

Did you know?
Muslims around the world eat special food in the month of Ramadan. What special food do you eat during this Holy month?

LAYLAT UL QADR

Laylat Ul Qadr is also known as the "Night of Power".
It is the night in Ramadan where the Quran was
revealed to our Beloved Prophet Muhammad (SAW).
This is a very important night for Muslims.

Circle the things we should do on this blessed night.
Hint! There are three things you can circle!

Did you know?
Laylat Ul Qadr is the night the Quran was revealed to the Prophet Muhammad (SAW)

THE NAMES OF ALLAH

Allah has 99 beautiful names.

Here are some below. Match the names by drawing a line from Allah's Arabic name to his name in English. Have a grown-up help you if you are stuck.

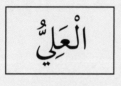 الْعَلِيُّ

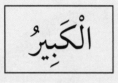 الْكَبِيرُ

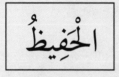 الْحَفِيظُ

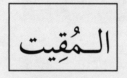 الْمُقِيت

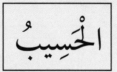 الْحَسِيبُ

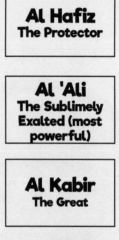

Al Hafiz
The Protector

Al 'Ali
The Sublimely Exalted (most powerful)

Al Kabir
The Great

Al Hasib
The Bringer of Judgement

Al Muqit
The Sustainer (provider)

"Allah has 99 names and whoever preserves them will enter paradise."

Helpful Hadith!

The Prophet Muhammad (SAW) said "if you learn the names of Allah, you will enter Paradise."
(Sahih al-Bukhari 7392, Sahih Muslim 2677)

ZAKAH

Zakah means charity. As Muslims, we must help the poor and needy. You can do this by giving money, helping the poor and people in need.

Can you help Omar & Hana figure out which is not a form of charity? Circle the action which is not a form of Zakah.

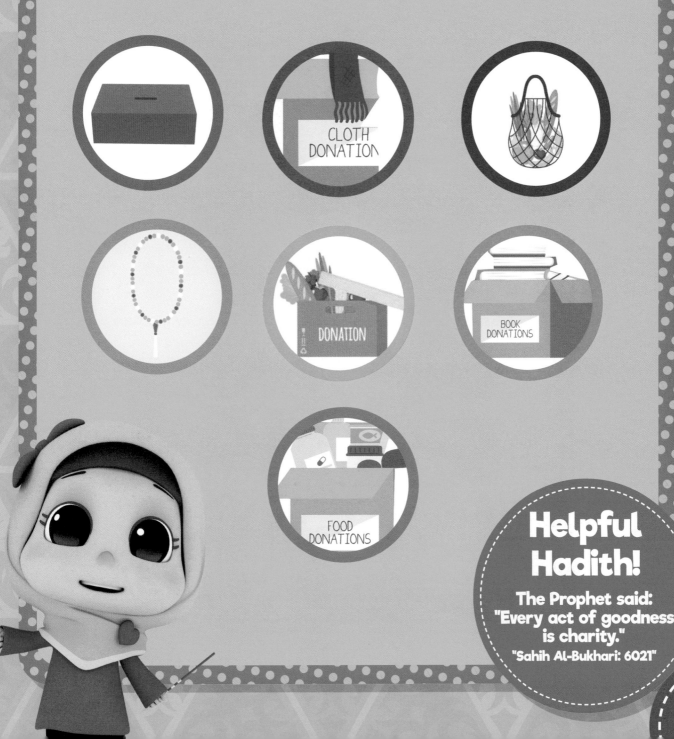

Helpful Hadith!

The Prophet said:
"Every act of goodness is charity."
"Sahih Al-Bukhari: 6021"

EID IS HERE! IT IS TIME TO CLEAN!

Can you help Omar make sure he has a clean room for Eid?
Spot the differences between the two image.

There are 5 differences to you to spot.

EID GREETINGS!

Can you help Omar & Hana design a Eid card?
With the help of an adult, fold an A4 piece of paper in half to create your very own Eid card. Design, colour and write your Eid card. Have a look below for some inspiration.
Use the stickers to make your card even better!

Did you know?
Eid al-Fitr means, "Festival of breaking fast."

DIY EID BUNTING

Omar & Hana need help designing and decorating a beautiful bunting for their home.

Draw and colour a special Eid Bunting in the template below. What else will you add?

Use lots of
bright colours!

Did you know?
Many Muslims around the house decorate
their homes for Eid. How will you
decorate your home?

37

CHOOSING NEW CLOTHES!

Help Omar & Hana with their brand-new Eid clothes.
Design and colour in Omar & Hana's clothes for Eid.
Be as creative as you can!

39

EID CELEBRATIONS!

Eid Mubarak! It's a Happy Day! Omar & Hana would love to know how you will be celebrating Eid.

Think about the following questions to help you create your poster: Who will you meet? What yummy food will you eat? What games will you play? What new clothes will you wear? Where will you go?

Did you know?
Eid - ul - Fitr is celebrated for 3 days.
How will you celebrate each day?